Santa Fe & Surrounds

John and Cassidy Olson
Photography by Olson Photographic LLC

Schiffer Publishing Ltd

4880 Lower Valley Road, Atglen, PA 19310 USA

John & Cassidy Olson
Library of Congress Control Number: 2005921975

Designed by Rick Perez
Type set in DomCasualBT

ISBN: 0-7643-2301-6
Printed in China

Published by Schiffer Publishing Ltd.
4880 Lower Valley Road
Atglen, PA 19310
Phone: (610) 593-1777; Fax: (610) 593-2002
E-mail: Info@schifferbooks.com

For the largest selection of fine reference books on this and related subjects, please visit our web site at www.schifferbooks.com
We are always looking for people to write books on new and related subjects. If you have an idea for a book please contact us at the above address.

This book may be purchased from the publisher.
Include $3.95 for shipping.
Please try your bookstore first.
You may write for a free catalog.

In Europe, Schiffer books are distributed by
Bushwood Books
6 Marksbury Ave.
Kew Gardens
Surrey TW9 4JF England
Phone: 44 (0) 20 8392-8585; Fax: 44 (0) 20 8392-9876
E-mail: info@bushwoodbooks.co.uk
Free postage in the U.K., Europe; air mail at cost.

Dedication & Acknowledgments

F.O.D. – Spencer, Cocoa, and Dante!

There are so many people we'd like to thank for their help, support, and contributions that we couldn't possibly name them all. However, a few people really stand out on this project. Robert and Joyce Olson for all their help and support while we are away from home base. Col. Eugene Leach and Elizabeth McClelland for all their enthusiasm and interest when we are excited about our ventures. Haynes - Our close friend and protégée, master of all – painter, electrician, landscape engineer, house sitter, dog sitter, arborist, and overall cool guy! Aside from taking pictures, we can't do much without him! Patty & Rose: The "kids" really appreciate your visits when we are away. Andy Frausini and all the great people at Pro Photo Gear: These people are the best! We get our equipment and supplies from them, but best of all, they have become our friends! Monique, Bruce, and Lavonne at Great Southwest Adventures: These people KNOW the Santa Fe area and were invaluable during our visit – we were sponges for their information and insights. J.J.: The very kind and distinguished gentleman working at the New Mexico Information Booth at the Albuquerque Airport. His enthusiasm and kind nature was contagious and set a wonderful first impression of the people of the "Land of Enchantment." Tammie Garcia who, from the comfort of her Connecticut home, rented a car for us as we waited in the Hertz line in the Albuquerque Sunport. We really could not have accomplished all we did without her assistance. Our editor, Tina Skinner, for this book would not have been possible without her trust and belief in us.

Contents

Chapter One
Hotels and Restaurants

Many of the hotels in Santa Fe offer dining as well as lodging. There are hundreds of places to stay in Santa Fe with something for every price range and expectation. Some places offer a full immersion into Southwestern living with true adobe architecture and furnishings, while others offer lodging with a Spanish colonial influence. Each restaurant offers its own specialties as well as twists on the old standards such as Huevos Rancheros and Chile Rellenos. Some restaurants offer a menu based on the food of the ancestral Puebloans, giving the customer a unique opportunity to dine in the present day and experience a taste of the past.

Flat roofed adobe architecture pairs beautifully with chile ristras for adornment.

The sign features an
adobe architecture
motif.

An adobe wall sections off the area from the street. Southwestern-style cutwork allows the light to shine in a pattern. Chile ristras complete the theme.

Sculpture helps to set off the sign and the architecture of The Inn and Spa at Loretto.

Adobe architecture at its best! Room-upon-room design borrows from the building patterns of the Pueblos.

HOTEL
ENTRANCE

The Hotel Santa Fe features the best of both worlds — ancient adobe architecture and modern windows.

The Hotel Santa Fe is owned by the people of the Picuris Pueblo. The interior
and the exterior both boast Southwest adobe styling.

An adobe wall separates the Hotel Santa Fe from the street. Many rooms have balconies to take in the view of downtown Santa Fe.

The roof of the entrance to La Posada de Santa Fe Resort and Spa is supported by heavy, peeled beams called *vigas*.

Above: Blending the architecture of Adobe, Mexican, Spanish, and Western creates an experience uniquely Santa Fe at the Hotel Plaza Real.

The Hotel Plaza Real offers shopping, lodging, and dining under one roof. Chiles adorn the porch.

Massive beams and timbers create a remarkable, and memorable, entrance to the Inn of the Anasazi.

The Inn of the Anasazi features elements of ancient pottery, stonework, and architecture to make it a unique place to stay or dine.

Chapter Two
Museums and Churches

Numerous museums are located within the Santa Fe city limits. Each is worth a visit, albeit even for a few moments. Even a brief visit is enough to impart some wisdom and perhaps ignite an interest in a particular subject. Santa Fe and the surrounding areas have churches everywhere! While it is interesting to stop to visit every one, and each is spectacular in its own way, a few stand out as stunning. From the miraculous stairway to the oldest church structure in the U.S.A., each church has an interesting story.

El Santuario de Chimayo, the Lourdes of America, gets visits from thousands of people who have heard the claim that it has healing powers in its soil.

The interior of the Santuario de Chimayo is quite beautiful and old. It was constructed between 1814 and 1816.

Legend has it that a monk in the Penitentes brotherhood saw a light coming from one of the hills near the Santa Cruz river. He unearthed a crucifix with his bare hands. A processional was organized to take the crucifix to Santa Cruz where it was put in the church. The next morning the crucifix had disappeared and was found back in its original location. After the third attempt to bring it to the church, it was decided that the crucifix wanted to stay in Chimayo, so a small chapel was built there.

Cigar trees and cottonwoods shade the outdoor chapel behind the Santuario de Chimayo.

The San Jose de Garcia Church in Las Trampas is an old adobe structure built in 1760. As with all adobe structures, it needs a fresh coat of mud every few years. Traditionally, it was the job of the village women to coat the church with mud from the local hillsides. Now workers are hired to perform such tasks. The church does not have electricity, so the candle candelabra is functional.

The ceiling is made of huge carved timbers. The floor is bare aged wood and the pews are simple with kneelers.

The sign in front of the San Miguel Church. There is some debate as to the true date of construction, but it is definitely worth a visit.

The beautiful San Miguel Church was built around 1610. Its thick walls and high windows made it an ideal place for protection during raids. Be sure to view what authorities say is the most splendid altar screen in the Southwest.

The Institute of American Indian Arts Museum dedicates itself to the display of native students' art and to training the next generation of museum professionals.

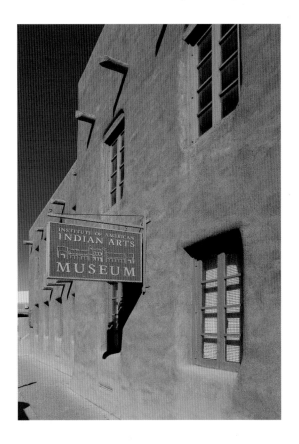

Located in downtown Santa Fe, The Institute of American Indian Arts Museum is easy to find and an essential part of any visit to Santa Fe. Read the rave reviews it has earned from both students and visitors.

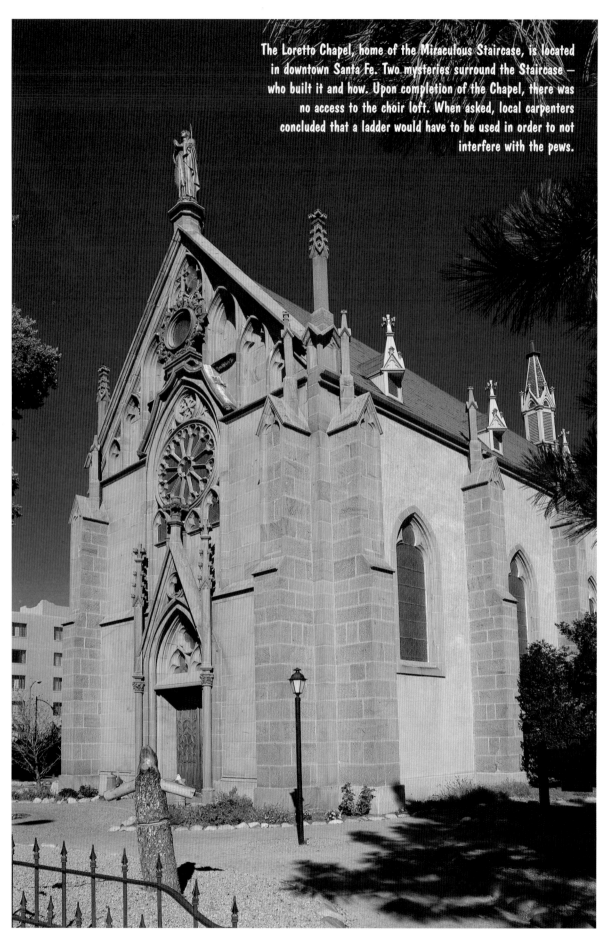

The Loretto Chapel, home of the Miraculous Staircase, is located in downtown Santa Fe. Two mysteries surround the Staircase — who built it and how. Upon completion of the Chapel, there was no access to the choir loft. When asked, local carpenters concluded that a ladder would have to be used in order to not interfere with the pews.

The Sisters of the Chapel made a novena to the patron saint of carpenters, Saint Joseph. On the ninth and last day of prayer, a man showed up at the chapel with a toolbox looking for work. After months of work, the staircase was complete and the carpenter could not be found. After a search for the mysterious man, many concluded that Saint Joseph himself built it.

The Palace of the Governors, the Museum of Indian Arts and Culture, the Museum of International Folk Art, the Museum of Fine Arts, and New Mexico State Monuments comprise the Museum of New Mexico.

The Museum of Fine Arts is one of the four museums of the Museum of New Mexico. It is the oldest museum for art in the state. The Museum of New Mexico predates New Mexican statehood.

MUSEUM OF FINE ARTS
MUSEUM OF NEW MEXICO

Blue sky and adobe architecture, the quintessence of New Mexico itself, come together in the Museum of New Mexico.

The flag of New Mexico flies proudly next to the Stars and Stripes. Yellow and red are the colors of Spain. The red sun on the yellow background features four rays within the four rays coming off the circle. The center circle is the circle of life and love, and the four rays within the four rays represent the four gifts of four bestowed upon the ancients: the four directions (North, East, South, West), the seasons (Winter, Spring, Summer, Fall), the day (Morning, Noon, Evening, Night), and a life (childhood, youth, middle years, and old age).

Formally called The Saint Francis of Assisi Church at Rancho de Taos, the church's new name is Ranchos de Taos Church. It is an adobe structure built with sun dried mud bricks and a layer of mud stucco. The architecture is stunning, the backside in particular, as it contains no windows or doors. Each year the church must have mud reapplied as rain wears it away slowly. Georgia O'Keefe immortalized it in a 1967 painting.

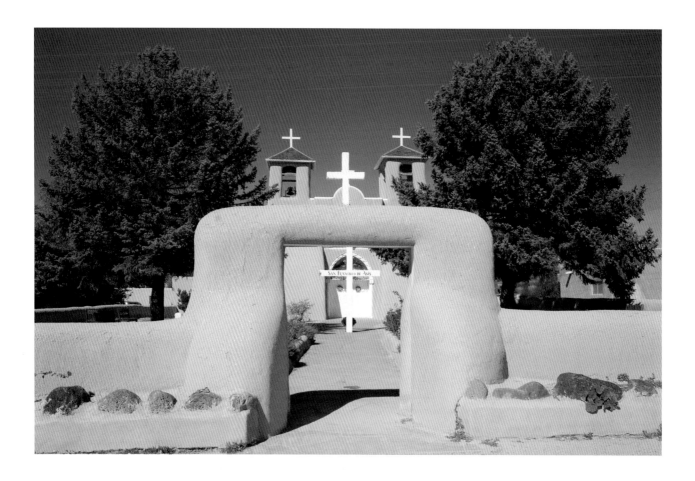

Once upon a time, the church was surfaced in cement, foolishly it turned out, to keep the adobe from wearing away. The rainwater leaked behind the cement and wore away the adobe underneath. Once the damage was discovered, the parishioners removed the cement and restored the church. The annual mudding began again quite joyfully as the church had been saved.

La Santa Rosa de Lima Church ruins with Pedernal in the background is an old adobe structure.

A chapel of the Penitentes sits at the foothills of Black Mesa and the Jemez Mountains. The Penitentes Brotherhood is a folk sect of Catholicism that acted as the lay priesthood when the priest would only visit once a year. As the years progressed, it became a mostly secret society of men who, to atone for their sins, practice flagellation and binding the body to a cross as in the crucification.

The Santuario de Guadalupe was built by Franciscan missionaries between 1776 and 1795 as a shrine to Our Lady of Guadalupe, the patron saint of Mexico. It currently houses the Archdiocese of Sante Fe's collection of carved images of the saints.

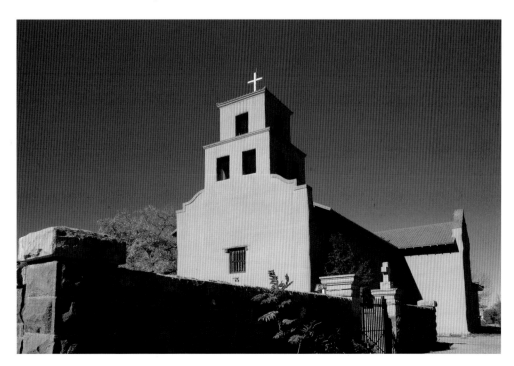

The construction of the Saint Francis Cathedral occurred over three centuries. The main adobe structure, the Conquistadora chapel, was built in 1714. The French-Romanesque cathedral was built later and commissioned in 1886. The Blessed Sacrament Chapel is a Modernist addition done in 1967. It is dedicated to Saint Francis of Assisi, the patron saint of Santa Fe.

The public is welcome to visit the Scottish Rite Temple, Monday through Friday. It is located in downtown Santa Fe.

The Cross of the Martyrs commemorates the deaths of 21 Franciscan friars and many Spanish Colonists during the Pueblo Revolt of 1680. The Pueblo Revolt of 1680 drove the Spaniards out of Indian lands and was the single most successful act of resistance of the Pueblos against a European invader. It was so successful that it forced religious toleration when the Spaniards returned. The cross and the kiva (traditional centers of worship) have co-existed peacefully ever since.

Chapter Three
Shops and Galleries

The place to be for a gallery is Canyon Road! Every art form imaginable is available for admiring and purchase on Canyon Road. It is a wonderful stroll on the Southeast side of the city. Make sure the Palace of the Governors receives attention as well as all the shops surrounding the downtown plaza.

The Palace of the Governors hosts 50 Indians selling their wares every day. There are only fifty and exactly fifty each day, even on Sunday. It is a lottery system from which names are drawn for each day. The jewelry is exquisite, distinctive, and varied.

A merchant hangs out his rugs for all to view.

Galisteo Street is lined with various shops and stores. Early in the morning the light is great for browsing . . . and buying!

Window shopping is a must in the downtown area of Santa Fe.

Parking is available on the street or in designated parking areas around downtown. Park and walk up and down each street to take in the local sites.

Sculpture in front of this gallery adds whimsy. The cowboy in front demands attention with his pistols while the cowboy behind him rides a bucking bronco.

Metal comes to life in the form of armadillos, cowboys, and other animals in front of this store. Tapestry adorns the adobe wall in the background.

Canyon Road, the street of galleries, is delineated by a large sign at either end. Galleries of paintings, sculptures, and anything artsy line this road. Walking down one side and up the other is a treat for the eyes.

A gallery on Canyon Road offers a taste of what is to come to the visitor upon entering.

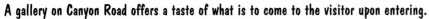

Beautiful landscaping envelopes this gallery, softening the adobe walls and massive windows.

Sculpture defines the garden area while advertising for this gallery. The moose stands demurely behind an adobe wall, while a cactus takes up residence nearby.

"Jesus said 'buy folk art'" according to a working studio on Canyon Road.

Desert vegetation and blue sky set this shop dramatically in the Santa Fe landscape.

The plaza in downtown Santa Fe is surrounded by shops, restaurants, and the Palace of the Governors. Shop and eat, then relax on the benches near the monument.

A beautiful structure with adobe walls and beams protruding for the roof is a picturesque setting for a future gallery or business.

Chapter Four
Plant life

Various desert animals depend and thrive on the vegetation in Santa Fe. On a lucky day, a roadrunner will fly by and dart into the brush alongside the highway. Look quickly, they are REALLY fast! By contrast, the Ponderosa and Piñon pine trees are stately and will wait patiently to be viewed. Stop to smell the sagebrush and the bark of the Ponderosa pine. A drive up to the Santa Fe Ski Basin may bring surprises on the way down — startled mule deer may run up a 70-degree incline providing entertainment. On the drive to Taos, a coyote may be wandering along the Rio Grande sipping from the river and enjoying the warmth of the sun.

The desert is home to many types of unique vegetation. This cactus was seen growing along the side of the road.

A cactus is in bloom.

Sunflowers add drama, color, and texture to the desert landscape.

Prickly pear cactus produce an edible fruit sold in markets as "tuna." The paddles of the cactus are edible as well.

Sage brush exists happily in New Mexico. It is extremely drought tolerant and hardy. It has a strong scent that can be overwhelming. Even hungry cattle won't eat it!

Mullen is a biennial that produces leaves its first year. It flowers, seeds, then dies in its second year.

Hollyhocks are a great old garden standby. They thrive well in the Southwest, as they need full sun.

The Ponderosa pine can live to be 400 years old. Because of their height, they are often victims of lightening damage. If the lightening does not strike them directly, any low intensity forest fire caused by it is good for the health of the tree. The fires return valuable nutrients to the soil and remove underbrush that steals water. On a hot day or when sunlight warms the tree bark, it smells of vanilla.

The Single Berry juniper is an important evergreen as it can withstand poor soil conditions and is very hardy. Unfortunately, they cannot withstand any forest fire and are the first to perish.

The Piñon tree is the official tree of New Mexico. The fruit of the Piñon tree is the Piñon nut or the pine nut. It is popular in gourmet cuisine in many cultures.

Cottonwoods are the indicator of the real gold in New Mexico — water. They grow where they can "get their feet wet" along streams and rivers. Seeds lay in the soil under the mature trees and wait for the spring thaw to flood the rivers and overflow their banks. Lack of flooding makes it hard for the seedlings to become established.

Aspen trees prefer higher elevations than the cottonwood trees. These aspens have settled in for the winter, awaiting spring.

Chapter Five
Natural Wonders

Upon landing at the airport, either Santa Fe or Albuquerque, the first observation is how different the landscape is, especially from the North or East. Ancient volcanoes and tectonic plate movement in conjunction with rain and wind have created landscape that truly is art. One cannot help but revel in the beauty of the harsh climate.

Cottonwoods create a yellow ribbon on the landscape in the fall announcing the presence of water.

Pines and evergreens stand sentinel in the Carson National Forest. The Rocky Mountains are in the background in the distance.

The eruption of the Valle Caldera millions of years ago rained down lava and ash over the landscape. As the lava and ash cooled, tuff (soft, crumbly rock) and welded tuff (rock harder than tuff) formed.

Vegetation keeps the soil from washing away in violent rain storms. Where there is no vegetation, the soil erodes.

The cottonwood trees indicate the presence of a stream.

Gentle hills and harsh rocks characterize the Santa Fe countryside.

Wondrous land formations glow as a storm approaches.

The striping on the red rocks is a result of millions of years of shifting between a lake bed and a marsh. Water, mineral deposits, and mud created a stripe each time the land would flood, then subsequently dry out.

The geological striping on this land formation is fantastic and has been in the making for millions of years on the outskirts of Santa Fe, near Abiquiu.

The geological striping continues for as far as the eye can see.

The Red Rocks section of New Mexico begins in the town of Abiquiu, north of Santa Fe. The landscape was created by completely different geological activity as compared to other areas of New Mexico.

Near Abiquiu, the red rocks of New Mexico resemble other geological areas, such as the Painted Desert in Arizona, more closely than the volcanic rock formations in Santa Fe.

Water and wind continue to change the landscape and structure.

A land formation on the rim of the Parajito Plateau
in the Jemez Mountains is sculpture in itself.

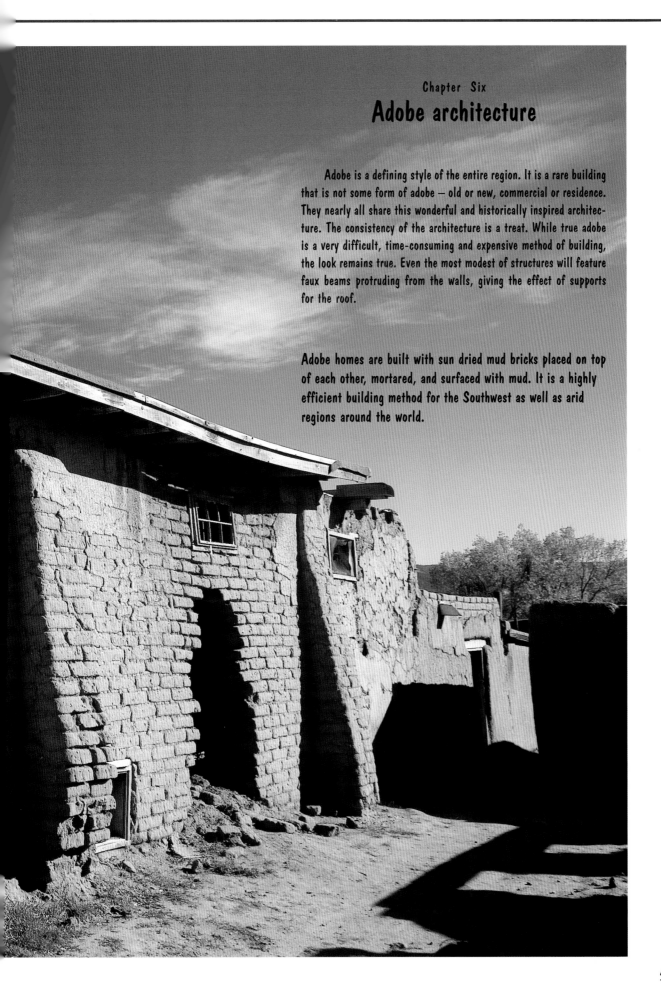

Chapter Six
Adobe architecture

Adobe is a defining style of the entire region. It is a rare building that is not some form of adobe — old or new, commercial or residence. They nearly all share this wonderful and historically inspired architecture. The consistency of the architecture is a treat. While true adobe is a very difficult, time-consuming and expensive method of building, the look remains true. Even the most modest of structures will feature faux beams protruding from the walls, giving the effect of supports for the roof.

Adobe homes are built with sun dried mud bricks placed on top of each other, mortared, and surfaced with mud. It is a highly efficient building method for the Southwest as well as arid regions around the world.

As the walls increase in height, they decrease slightly in
thickness due to the weight of the bricks on the ones below.
The bricks are mostly uniform in shape. Corners and walls
are strengthened with additional bricks.

The mud bricks and the mud walls create fanciful designs and allow for ornamentation on a gateway in Taos.

The Mabel Dodge Luhan home is a classic example of Southwest styling and use of adobe. Dodge was a socialite who made New Mexico her home in 1916. She fell in love with Taos, and with Antonio Luhan, a full-blooded pueblo man. Her home is now open to the public as a bed and breakfast, retreat, and conference center.

Adobe structures must have mud reapplied every few years to keep the surface in tiptop shape and looking beautiful. Some of the mud is washed away with each rain shower. Some buildings show more wear on the upper surfaces where the rain has pounded pieces of mud away. With each additional layer of mud applied, an adobe house grows!

Views of the landscape and various homes built into it surround downtown Santa Fe.

Even the birds build with adobe! Many kinds of birds use mud for their nests, including house martins, blackbirds, and swallows.

Long and low homes are a common sight in Santa Fe. The homes blend into the landscape instead of rising like a spire into the sky, as with architecture in other parts of the United States.

Elaborate details on the roofline draw the eye up. The windows are covered with decorative shutters painted a beautiful shade that compliments the adobe walls. Hedges complete the view.

Windows are set into the walls. The adobe wall is at least two feet thick. With each mudding, the wall grows a few inches, making the home incredibly efficient.

Landscaping softens the adobe wall in front of this home.

An adobe wall with fencing must be placed around any utilities, such as air conditioners or heat pumps, to preserve the architectural beauty of Santa Fe. These fences are derived from "coyote fences" used in more rural areas. Traditionally, settlers used the skinny parts of trees to create tall fences to keep coyotes out and livestock in and safe. Now they are mainly used for decoration and to protect utilities.

Mailboxes are set into the adobe wall and create an interesting visual that is uniquely Santa Fe.

Turquoise trim mimics the sky and reminds the viewer that this colorful stone has been mined throughout New Mexico. The hanging chiles and landscaping are distinctly Southwest.

The vines break up the linear architecture and coordinate colors perfectly.

Far Left: Heavy beams support the roof. Hedges soften the harsh corners of the walls. The door is framed beautifully by the soft color of the adobe mud walls.

Left: A mailbox adds interest to a wall.

Below: Dappled shade from cottonwood trees casts shadows on an interesting doorway.

Beautiful trim accents the window. Upon reapplication of the adobe mud, a building can acquire fabulous texturing.

Terra cotta pots sit on the front porch. A beautiful deciduous tree provides much needed shade during the heat of the summer.

The door is functional and wonderfully styled. Note the enormous timbers creating the doorframe. The door is set into the wall and is completely surrounded by mud.

By contrast, cut timbers create the top of the door frame and the mud wall does not encase the door.

A brilliant blue door topped with a heavy painted timber provides contrast
against the reddish color of the adobe mud.

A door allows entry into the courtyard created by the wall on one side and the house on the other.

A fantastic arch crowns this double door.

Adobe homes sit at the foot of massive stone formations. An enormous volcanic explosion millions of years ago in conjunction with millions of years of weather created the landscape of today.

Chapter Seven
Surrounding Santa Fe

A visit to Santa Fe is not complete without side trips to Taos, Bandelier National Monument where the ancestral Puebloans' cave dwellings are preserved, and Abiquiu, home of the world famous painter, Georgia O'Keefe. The mountains are massive, enjoyable and unmistakable!

The Jemez Mountains form the southernmost tip of the Rocky Mountains. They rose as a result of volcanic activity millions of years ago.

In the foreground, desert grasses grow with evergreens. Cotton-woods rise beyond indicating water. The foothills are dotted with trees. A magnificent view of the Jemez Mountains tops the photo as they meet the sky.

The blast of a volcano 1.5 million years ago was 600 times larger than the eruption of Mount St. Helen's in 1980. Lava runs and ash covered the landscape. Water and weather have worn away the softer material, leaving massive rock formations.

The Jemez Mountains are in view beyond. Cottonwoods prove the existence of water nearby.

Over time, with the help of water, the softer volcanic ash has eroded. Mesas and ridges that appear to be in the form of fingers remain.

Runoff from the mountain snows feed the rivers. Cottonwoods depend on the runoff to sustain them.

The band of gold is cottonwood trees in their autumnal glory, set against the Jemez Mountains.

The Sangre de Cristo Mountains, translation "Blood of Christ," are appropriately named as they glow red at sunset. The Sangre de Cristo Mountains are part of the Southern Rocky Mountains and they include the Santa Fe Mountains and the Truchas Mountains. Legend has it that blood was actually shed for Christ by the Penitentes in secret crucifixions.

The city of Santa Fe is 7,000 feet above sea level. It is encircled by the Sangre de Cristo Mountains, part of the Rocky Mountains.

Low rolling hills and vegetation frame a distant view of the Sangre de Cristo Mountains.

From downtown Santa Fe, there are fabulous views of the Sangre de Cristo Mountains.

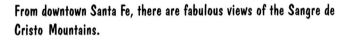

At an elevation of 12,175 feet above sea level, Ski Santa Fe is located within the Santa Fe National Forest.

The Truchas Mountains, translation "trout mountains," provided much needed runoff from the melting snow in the spring. The mountains provide great trout fishing, hence the name.

Imagine moving across the United States to the settle the west. Imagine a vast stretch of flat land in front and the mountains behind. Imagine trying to cover 12 to 15 miles a day In a covered wagon with horses. The gorge is Just outside of Taos, Just to the Northwest of town.

The Rio Grande Gorge is accessible by a dirt road. It is steep and slow, but worth the drive. A drive through it gives a true appreciation of the size and power of Mother Nature.

A storefront in Taos invites shopping and browsing. Make sure to take a stroll down Bent Street, named for Governor Bent who was murdered in 1847 in his home by an angry mob protesting American rule.

Colorful tapestry rugs hang in Taos. Both Santa Fe and Taos are highly artistic areas and feature the works of many locals.

Shops and galleries line the plaza in Taos.

The Kit Carson house and museum is located in Taos and worth a visit. Kit Carson, one of America's great frontiersmen, arrived in Santa Fe from Missouri in 1826. He used Taos as a base camp for fur-trapping expeditions from 1828 to 1831.

The Taos Plaza has benches and large trees to provide respite and shade from the hot Southwest sun.

A beautifully carved ornate sign announces the Taos Plaza.

The Taos Pueblo reservation is in the foothills of the Sangre de Cristo Mountains. In 1970, the Federal Government returned 48,000 acres of mountain land to the Taos Pueblo. Blue Lake, a sacred place for religious ceremonies, was part of the parcel and is once again part of the spiritual and cultural fabric that defines the Taos Pueblo.

A stream separates the North house (Hlauuma) and the South house (Hlaukwima). Both houses are adobe structures and have no electricity or running water. Life in the North or South houses is designed to maintain cultural traditions despite the "modernization" of the surrounding areas.

A view of the Taos Pueblo plaza reveals the vastness of the adobe homes. Only the doors are new. Access was traditionally through the roof via a ladder. The ladder was pulled in to keep intruders at bay. The hole in the roof was covered by a piece of wood to protect the occupants from the elements.

The Pueblo (Spanish meaning "village") is built entirely of adobe. It is actually many homes with adjoining walls — highly efficient construction! While the walls are connected, there are no doors between homes.

The landscape of Abiquiu is inspiring. The most famous artist to be inspired by this wondrous scenery was Georgia O'Keefe. She made her home here and painted the surrounding areas.

The skull is a reoccurring theme in New Mexico. It is a frequent motif of Georgia O'Keefe's paintings.

The Abiquiu Inn is a great place to stop for lunch or dinner after exploring the Abiquiu landscape and sites.

The home of famed artist Georgia O'Keefe (1887-1986) sits on the hillside and overlooks the Abiquiu landscape. O'Keefe purchased her Abiquiu home in 1945. In 1989 the Georgia O'Keefe Foundation took over the property to maintain and preserve it as a tribute to her. It is open to the public on a limited basis, by appointment only.

The Abiquiu landscape is dominated by Cerro Pedernal. The Abiquiu reservoir is in front of it. It boasts some of the finest fishing in Northern New Mexico. Swimming is the most popular form of recreation, although people do water and jet ski.

Cottonwood trees punctuate the Abiquiu landscape, in contrast with the Red Rocks in the distance.

An approaching storm allows the sun to peek through and illuminate the Red Rocks.

The Rio Chama begins north of Abiquiu. It flows south, past Abiquiu, and meets the Rio Grande. It is a major tributary of the Rio Grande and parts of it are designated wilderness study areas.

The Rio Chama flows along, completely unaware of its impact on people. Water rights are a big deal in New Mexico — any land with rights to river water carries a premium over other parcels. Irrigation is done by flooding the land, as it has been for a hundred years, making it a "tradition" difficult to break despite its inefficiencies.

The entire Chama Valley can be viewed while driving State Highway 84.

Cottonwood trees grow along the Rio Chama.

Ghost Ranch has been the scene of numerous Hollywood films. The cabin was built for the movie, *City Slickers*.

Cliff dwellings were homes for the ancestral Puebloans. Many area Pueblo people are believed to be descendants. The cliffs were formed from volcanic ash. Water and wind wore away the stone forming holes. The holes in the cliffs were often hollowed out by the Puebloans to create larger areas.

All that remains of the old store rooms in the village dwelling are the brick foundations. Parts of Bandelier National Monument have been reconstructed to give a sense of the past and explain how people lived.

The kiva, or ceremonial room, was once underground. Many Pueblo traditions link their people to the earth as having risen out of it from a spirit hole.

A view of the cliff dwellings from a distance gives one pause. The drama of the cliffs and the sheer number of residences means this was a happening place.

This cave was home to someone in history. The painted art is now protected from the elements by a clear covering.

Bandelier National Monument was designated to preserve archeological sites in the Jemez Mountains. It is named after Adolph F. A. Bandelier, a self-taught anthropologist/historian. This view is of the village on the floor of the Frijoles Canyon.

A reconstructed adobe home sits in front of a cave, effectively expanding the home site. The cliffs are very soft and can be worn away by water or pressure. Timbers were routinely pounded and twisted into the cliff's side to anchor the roof of a stone home in front of a cave.

The line of holes in the cliffs indicates cave dwellings.

The Rito de los Frijoles — translated to Little Bean Creek — runs through the Frijoles Canyon. It is suspected that there was a drought so severe that the river no longer flowed. No water meant that the crops failed and the inhabitants were forced to leave.

The ancestral Puebloans lived and worked all along
Frijoles Canyon. Only a small section has been
excavated, but the cave dwellings are as far as the eye
can see from this vantage point.

The sculpture celebrating flight and a connection to the ancient traditions greets everyone upon arrival at the Albuquerque Sunport.

May no one forget how aviation was born. In a similar fashion, the Pueblo consciously work to keep their traditions alive and unforgotten.

Chapter Eight
Of Interest: Santa Fe

The region holds many points of interest as noted in the previous chapters. Some additional areas to note are the Carson National Forest, the Veterans National Cemetery, and the city of Los Alamos — an area that is still a very scientific community to this day. While visiting all the areas of Santa Fe, there are more discreet details that help define the region — chiles ristras, the ditch system of irrigation, and the remains of old adobe structures that serve as a reminder of a simpler time gone by. Beauty exists all around Santa Fe — experience it!

Painted highway bridges infuse local culture and add interest to the landscape. Each bridge has the name of a Pueblo, modern or ancient, inscribed in it.

Various native wildlife are depicted on overpasses and along highway retaining walls. Bulls are pictured on this particular bridge but images of roadrunners, snakes, turkeys, lizards, and rabbits also appear.

The Veterans National Cemetery is located on the western side of Santa Fe.

Rows of white markers pay final tribute to those who have served.

Fanciful sculpture is all around the Santa Fe area. These wonderful people were outside a Chimayo weaving studio.

A blown glass sculpture catches the light and calls out to viewers.

Glassblowing is an active art in Shidoni in Tesuque, on the outskirts of Santa Fe.

The entrance to Shidoni is marked with sculpture. The grounds are actually a gallery for sculpture.

SHIDONI

GALLERY

PLEASE NO DOGS

ALL BUSES

The ditch system runs through neighborhoods providing water. Each person must take only what he is entitled to so enough remains to provide for those down the water line.

Water is a scarce resource in New Mexico. The average yearly rainfall in Santa Fe is eight inches. The landscape is heavily dependent on the runoff from mountain snows. A running stream means life can continue on as it has for centuries.

The ditch system brings water from rivers and streams to farms and neighborhoods. If a parcel of land has water rights, the owners are assigned a time slot for water receipt. When the time comes, a door to the ditch is opened and water floods the land. Everyone with water rights is responsible for the upkeep of the ditch. If someone decides to not take an interest in the ditch, he may be rewarded with a terrible time slot (3AM).

Ingenious gutter design helps capture rain water and funnel it into waiting rain barrels. Water can then be saved for a sunny day.

Above: The water meter is an integral part of the downtown Santa Fe landscape. Below: Santa Fe National Forest has rolling hills and evergreen, as well as deciduous trees.

Buy summer vegetables when buying chile ristras.

Chile ristras, both large and small, are available for sale at roadside stands.

Ring for service to purchase these chiles. Once they dry, make chile sauce!

"But it's dry heat!" The skull serves as a reminder to take precautions in the desert.

Bird condos under shade trees provide year round shelter. Santa Fe is desert and daily temperatures get extremely hot. However, every night the land cools to about 50 degrees Fahrenheit for comfortable resting.

Sunset in Santa Fe is art that surrounds the viewer. As the sun slips slowly behind the mountains, the changing sky and landscape create a daily masterpiece. As night falls, the city lights illuminate "The City Different."

Other Great Books on the Southwest, from Schiffer Books

The Navajo Art of Sandpainting. *Revised & Expanded 2nd Edition*. Douglas Congdon-Martin. Sandpainting has it origin in the religious tradition and practice of the Navajo people. It forms a central part of their religious chants, being a place where Earth People and Holy People come into harmony, giving healing and protection. Sandpainting is understood as being very powerful, and for many years it was deemed unwise and even dangerous not to erase the paintings when the ritual was completed. In the course of the twentieth century this attitude has modified allowing for many representations to be made, while still not violating the religious traditions. Sandpainting thus have come to be an internationally appreciated and collected art form.

In this newly revised and expanded volume, over 400 sandpaintings are illustrated in full color. They range from the most traditional to the new forms that are being developed today. The sandpaintings are organized by artist, making this an important reference for collectors.
Size: 8 1/2" x 11" • 346 color photos • 64 pp.
ISBN: 0-7643-0810-6 • soft cover • $9.95

The Hopi Approach to the Art of Kachina Doll Carving. Erik Bromberg. The beautiful diversity of Hopi Kachina dolls is pictorially presented to show past, present, and evolving styles. These carved representations of ceremonial figures taking part in celebration of the Kachina religion are highly collected by Indian and white peoples alike.

This book serves to explain, compare, and present the variety of dolls that are found through color pictures, line drawings and a concise text.

The carvers are given a great deal of recognition throughout the book as the discussion covers the environment, tools, and prominence of these artists. An appendix lists 495 living artists. An introduction is by Frederick Dockstader, former director to the Museum of the American Indian in New York.

Mr. Bromberg, a trader among the Hopi, shares his accumulated respect for the culture and people who produce them. His chapters evolved to answer questions by collectors and gallery workers. The result is a first-hand analysis of this contemporary and still changing art form that has both religious and commercial impact on the Hopi carvers. Only a trusted, sympathetic student of the Hopi culture could have compiled the background interpretations of the dolls and won the respect of the carvers.
Size: 8 1/2" x 11" • 164 photos & drawings • 94 pp.
ISBN: 0-88740-062-0 • soft cover • $9.95

Native American Fetishes. Kay Whittle. When is a fetish not a fetish? Find out in this celebration of the most misunderstood genre of Southwestern Indian carvings. From Beast Gods to Directional Guardian Spirits, this book explores the magic and mystery behind the charismatic, mostly stone, animal figures or fetishes skillfully carved by artists from the Southwestern Pueblos. Enthusiasts will delight in the hundreds of full-color photographs. Pictures and text highlight the impressive variety of forms, materials, and traditional and contemporary styles available to collectors. This book discusses the symbolic meanings associated with these figures and explains how they are "borrowed" for use by members of non-Native American cultures. A price guide is included to help collectors orient themselves to current market values.
Size: 6 1/2" x 9" • 313 photos • 160 pp.
ISBN: 0-7643-0429-1 • soft cover • $14.95